ABANDONING EGYPT

DARE TO MOVE:
21 Days to Overcoming Stagnation
and Getting Unstuck Devotional

Lorraine Murray-Richardson

WESTBOW
PRESS®
A DIVISION OF THOMAS NELSON
& ZONDERVAN

WestBow Press books may be ordered through booksellers or by contacting:

WestBow Press
A Division of Thomas Nelson & Zondervan
1663 Liberty Drive
Bloomington, IN 47403
www.westbowpress.com
844-714-3454

Interior Image Credit: Author Photo by Derrys A. Richardson

ISBN: 979-8-3850-2487-2 (sc)
ISBN: 979-8-3850-2488-9 (hc)
ISBN: 979-8-3850-2489-6 (e)

Library of Congress Control Number: 2024908777

Print information available on the last page.

WestBow Press rev. date: 05/28/2024

CONTENTS

DEDICATION

I dedicate this book to the following people:

- To the people worldwide who find themselves stuck in any situation: May your rescue arrive swiftly, and may you courageously take the first step toward freedom.
- To my dear husband, James Maurell: You have been my unwavering support when I needed it the most, always displaying patience and grace. You will forever hold a special place in my heart.
- To my lovely daughter, Maura-Monee: Thank you for guiding me on this profound faith journey, especially when I doubted in moments of fear. Continue to inspire your generation with your fearless faith and unwavering commitment to God's loving heart.
- To my adoring son, Morgan Maurell: "Mom, your job is in your dreams, so go ahead and dream it," you gently reminded me one morning, curious about the contents of my dream. Your wise words resonated deeply. May you grow into the extraordinary man of God I envisioned in my dreams before you were born.
- To Shanelle Giraud: Your friendship has filled my life with love and security. I am grateful for everything you have done for me. I cherish you incredibly.
- To Living Hope Cathedral: Thank you for embracing my children as nieces and nephews and allowing them to find a family within your congregation. Your love and support are invaluable, and I will forever hold you dear in my heart.

FOREWORD

Lorraine Murray-Richardson and I have been married for twenty-two years. She has always loved books, so it is no surprise that she aspired to write her own. Lorraine's most notable characteristics are her perseverance and commitment. Her devotion to her work is evident in her prayers for our family and others. She wants to live for God and encourages others to do the same. Lorraine is not the type to give up easily; she believes even when there is nothing left to believe. As a result, when she said that God wanted her to resign from her job after fifteen years, I was initially hesitant.

Nonetheless, I realized that walking alongside her in obedience was critical. "Abandoning Egypt" was inspired by God. I like reading it and having it read to me. As a result, I have let go of ideas that had been imprisoning me for years. I applaud her efforts and hope this is the first of many books expressing her desire to see others live passionately for Christ.

James M. Richardson

PREFACE

Daily, discontent fills the air as people pour out their frustrations about their jobs, relationships, communities, health, government, and religious settings. The persistence of unresolved grievances often results in a lack of proactive action, frequently leaving those issues unaddressed or unfairly thrust upon individuals who lack the power or willingness to help. Theodore Roosevelt's words echo truthfully amidst this chorus of complaints. He defined whining as "complaining about a problem without offering a solution." I, too, have succumbed to the attraction of complaining about various facets of life. Whether it was the ongoing challenges at work, the chaos that invaded my sanctuary at home, the demands of raising children, or the continuous strain on my financial well-being, I became ensnared in the trap of discontent. Fear wrapped around my heart, hindering me from seeking solutions that could set me free.

Consequently, I endured toxic situations simply because some positivity was present in my life. Perhaps a beloved relative lived nearby, or a significant other sent flowers to commemorate a special occasion, or maybe the attraction of a competitive salary clouded my vision. Amid these occasional glimmers, the weight of negativity often eclipsed any flicker of hope. Oh, the comfort of wallowing in despair and enduring the fruitless pangs of suffering rather than summoning the courage to embark on the journey of self-improvement. In this wild state, my perspective underwent a transformative shift inspired by a profound exploration of Exodus in the Bible. A revelation stirred within me as I read through the pages, absorbing the chronicle of the Israelites' plight, their arrival in Egypt, their eventual settlement, and their breathtaking Exodus. I realized that, like those ancient wanderers, I, too, had been trapped in the cycle of whining, ignorant of the divine promise of deliverance promised to me. The pages of Exodus became a rallying cry, a spiritual wake-up call urging me to acknowledge God's willingness to guide and assist me. From this revelation, the seeds of change blossomed into the creation of this devotion known as "Abandoning Egypt." "This transformative book serves as a reminder that God, the compassionate listener, hears our anguished cries, comprehends our deepest sorrows, and has already begun freeing us."

"But first, we must be willing to let go of whatever is holding us back, whether it is people, things, or wrong beliefs. Experience the powerful blend of faith within this narrative by reading it daily for twenty-one days to fully realize its impact immediately and allow for transformation and the breaking of harmful habits. Freedom awaits you to carry you towards the promised land beyond the confines of your personal Egypt, that temporary haven of bondage. Moreover, do not overlook the strength of the affirmations in this book. They can fill you with resilience and motivation, no matter your challenges. Embrace them fully, build upon their meaning, and confidently repeat them daily—God's promises will become your reality.

Furthermore, take time to respond to thought-provoking questions, participate in reflection and gratitude exercises, activate the call to change, and engage in sincere prayer aligned with your deepest aspirations. Remember, do not underestimate God's ability to respond, just as He did for the Israelites. He is ready to hear and act on your heartfelt prayers. With steadfast faith, you can conquer any obstacle in your way.

ACKNOWLEDGMENT

I am grateful to Jehovah EL ROI for seeing me.
May I always be able to cling to him!

"OUT OF EGYPT,
I CALLED MY SON."

Liz's question, "Are you sure you are not in Egypt?" echoed persistently in my thoughts like a stubborn melody that never ends. Contemplating her words, I discovered a connection between historical Egypt as depicted in the Bible and my journey. What once seemed merely a distant backdrop transformed into a compelling symbol, mirroring my struggles and fervent pursuit of freedom. The mockery of being in Egypt was both painful and thought-provoking, sparking a fire within me to explore my circumstances and find a way out. Drawing inspiration from the stories of Abraham, Sarah, and Jesus, who sought refuge in Egypt, I delved deeper into the symbolism and lessons rooted in their experiences. Like them, I sought shelter, comfort, and stability in "My Egypt" - a job at a local agency. However, it had become a self-imposed exile, stifling my growth and potential.

On May 24, 2019, I decided to break free from the chains of "My Egypt." With a heart filled with uncertainty and a resignation letter tightly clutched in my hands, I arrived at work before the break of dawn. Stealthily, I slipped the resignation letter under my boss's door, hoping to avoid the questions that would surely follow. It was a bold move, defying the expectations imposed by family and society, insisting that I should not leave this job until I had another lined up. Leaving behind the security I had known for fifteen long years, doubts crept in. The absence of a clear plan or a new job opportunity made it challenging to explain why I had chosen this path to my family and friends. They saw it as an ill-timed leap into the unknown, and I struggled to convince them otherwise.

Nevertheless, deep down, I knew God directed me to trust Him, step into the wilderness, and rely on His guidance. As months passed, my faith dwindled. The promising interviews I had attended failed to materialize into tangible opportunities, leaving me with dwindling funds and a disheartened family. During moments of despair, I admitted to myself the need for clarity and direction. Seeking solace in prayer and fasting, I immersed myself in the scriptures. One day, I stumbled upon Isaiah 31:1 through deliberate reading, a passage conveying a profound message of caution and hope. It reminded me that looking to the world for help and relying on human strength alone was parallel to seeking refuge in Egypt, a futile endeavor. Returning to my old job, despite its familiarity, would only perpetuate this cycle of bondage. With this newfound understanding, I embarked on a quest to comprehend the Exodus story more deeply. The Exodus was not merely a historical account but a transformative narrative of overcoming obstacles, embracing trust, and stepping into a new beginning. I recognized this as my journey brimmed with challenges and uncertainties. Fear, panic, and worry accompanied me on this path; however, I embraced them as companions rather than adversaries. They reminded me of the courage it took to leave my personal Egypt and venture into the unknown. Just as God led the Israelites out of Egypt, He guided me through my trials, whispering words of encouragement and opening doors of opportunity. Despite setbacks, I remained steadfast in believing this journey led me towards a greater purpose. Looking towards the horizon, I invite others to join me on this journey to freedom. Together, let us break free from the shackles of our Egypt, cast aside the limitations imposed upon us, and embark on a new path of freedom and fulfillment. In the wilderness lies the promise of transformation, and with faith, we shall conquer the challenges and arrive at our promised land.

WEEK 1- DAY 1

Unlocking Your Egypt:
"Discovering and Escaping Limiting Patterns"

*"Be careful that you do not forget the Lord, who brought
you out of Egypt, out of the land of slavery."*
Deuteronomy 6:12

What is your Egypt? (a job, relationship, family, etc.)

_____

_____

_____

Navigating the complexities of my job at a local facility, which I now refer to as My-Egypt, posed a unique challenge. It served as a sanctuary that gave me a sense of purpose and a lifeline to support and sustain my household. However, in the shadows of this sanctuary, I could feel the subtle grip of entrapment tighten around me. The walls of my workplace, once a source of inspiration and growth, now felt like an inescapable prison. What was once a place of purpose and ambition had transformed into an oppressive environment that left me feeling trapped.

I did not always recognize this job as My-Egypt but as a Goshen, a little haven of comfort. Initially, it was an exciting adventure, an opportunity to embrace adulthood and responsibility. I was enthusiastic, fueled by the prospects of my first real job and the promise of a leadership role. Little did I know that behind the shiny surface lurked a maze of problems that led to constant conflicts, work-life imbalances, burnout, and a toxic corporate culture. I knew I had to break free from its clutches, but it was more complicated than I expected. This decision marked my second resignation, the first being when I outgrew my position at a doctor's office I had held since high school. Although the situations may appear similar, the first departure, without a backup plan, carried a lighter burden. I had minimal financial responsibilities, only one child, and a modest savings account. This time around, though, the stakes were higher. I had a mortgage looming over me, school tuition to pay, student loans to shoulder, two young children to care for, and aging parents in need of support.

The need for a job became a pressing need. "Anything will do," I half-heartedly joked with my friend Mel. Sensing my distress, she advised, "Remember, interviews are a two-way street. Do not forget to interview those who are interviewing you." I agreed but was preoccupied with the upcoming interview at a prestigious company. Given the environment of hiring freezes and limited employment prospects, this job opportunity held significant importance for me.

Regardless of responsibilities or compensation, I was determined to accept the offer. However, fate had other plans, and I bombed the interview. As I sat there, my heart was pounding, and anxiety and worry gripped my mind. I could not help but wonder if the interview had been an utter disaster. Had I irreparably damaged my chances of finding a new job? How could I discern whether the feeling that urged me to leave my secure position was a divine message or a mere miscommunication? Amid this uncertainty, conflicting emotions swirled around me. Could it be true that this once-revered hospital, a sanctuary of healing and care, transformed into a metaphorical prison—unexpectedly gripping me in its bonds? Or have I allowed myself to delve too deeply into the circumstances, clouding my judgment with my perceptions? Could this be my very own Goshen, a miniature Egypt where I find myself, teeming with abundant blessings but suffering a temporary setback? Like the children of Israel enduring years of hardship before freedom, perhaps my journey is destined for a miraculous turnaround. Questions about God's involvement in my predicament plagued my thoughts. Was He dismissing me, like how He had seemingly forsaken the children of Israel for 400 years in Egypt? Did He not remember our shared history? He led me to this job, only to abandon me.

Soul Search

As you reflect on the challenges in your own life, consider the concept of your personal Egypt. What sanctuary, though once comforting, now feels confining? Explore your journey and the possibility of a miraculous turnaround, for sometimes, our most extraordinary transformations emerge from the depths of adversity. It is time to confront your Egypt—whether it is a person, a place, an idea, or something else entirely. Face it head-on, for only by acknowledging and challenging what holds us back can we find the freedom and fulfillment we seek.

Guided Prayer

Lord, I thank you for the reminder in Exodus 20:1-26 that you are the God who freed the Israelites from the shackles of Egypt, liberating them from their house of captivity. I acknowledge my shortcomings in recognizing the bonds that have trapped me, hindering me from embracing the freedom You offer. Please forgive me. Now, in this moment of reflection, I seek your guidance to confront the challenges that have held me captive. Illuminate the corners of my heart and mind, allowing me to honestly address each obstacle that has persisted for far too long._____

_____, (list obstacles) With your strength, I believe I can face and overcome these trials. Empower me with your wisdom and discernment to discern the steps needed to break free from these chains. Please grant me the courage to relinquish control and place my trust in your plan for my deliverance. May this journey of redemption testify to your unwavering grace and unfailing love, in Jesus' Name.

Affirmation

God is turning my situation around, and I am coming out on top.

Personalized Prayer and Reflection: [Your personalized prayer and reflection here]

_____

_____

_____

_____

_____

_____

_____

_____

_____

_____

_____

WEEK 1- DAY 2

Overstaying Your Welcome: "Knowing When to Say Goodbye"

"Then the LORD said to Abram, you can be sure that your descendants will be strangers in a foreign land, where they will be oppressed as slaves for 400 years."
Genesis 15:13

Why are you still Here? (fear, finances, family, loyalty, etc.)

_____

_____

_____

When the unexpected interview call interrupted my day, emotions consumed me. It was mid-morning, and I had just stepped into the cozy embrace of my favorite local bookstore to pick up a long-awaited book order and get caught up with any new books that may have caught my interest. When I received the most unexpected call from a member of the Human Resources team from a local facility, it seemed like I had applied for that job more than six months prior; however, the urgency in the human resource voice was intense as she candidly confessed her multiple failed attempts to reach me, emphasizing that this call was her final effort. Caught off guard, I could feel the weight of the situation pressing down on me. With only 30 minutes to make it to the interview, I knew I had no time to spare. Racing against the clock, I made a split-second decision to forego returning home to change into proper attire. Instead, I entered the interview room dressed in brown flip-flops and a lilac beach dress, feeling acutely out of place amidst the sea of well-dressed candidates in suits and polished shoes. Despite the odds stacked against me, I held onto a glimmer of hope. Miraculously, I secured the job. They say the rest is history, but the journey from that moment was far from ordinary.

Reflecting, my experience at "My-Egypt" mirrored the struggles of God's chosen people in Goshen. Nestled in the Delta region of Egypt, Goshen was a place of comfort and abundance for the Israelites, like my situation, where I found solace in familiarity despite the signs of toxicity and stagnation surrounding me. For over a year, I ignored the warning signs, dismissing them as mere inconveniences in a sea of complaints from those around me. The idea of leaving My-Egypt crossed my mind fleetingly, triggered by moments of frustration and discontent with the leadership's decisions. However, duty and obligation always prevailed, convincing me that My-Egypt needed me as much as I needed it. However, just as the Israelites were blind to their entrapment, so was I. It took time for me to realize that true liberation lay beyond the walls of complacency. The journey towards change was fraught with uncertainty and fear, but it was a journey I needed to undertake.

Soul Search

Perhaps, like me, you have found comfort in familiarity, even at the cost of your growth and happiness. Maybe you, too, have hesitated to step out of the confines of your own Goshen despite the signs pointing towards a greater, although uncertain, path. Consider the moments when you have felt the weight of duty and obligation pressing down on you, convincing you to stay in a situation that no longer serves you. Reflect on the times when you have brushed aside the whispers of change, dismissing them as mere inconveniences in the grand scheme. Really, why are you still here?

Guided Prayer

Heavenly Father, I come before You humbly, seeking Your guidance and understanding during challenging circumstances. Grant me the clarity to see how these situations have impacted my relationship with You and others. Help me to recognize the importance of prioritizing my connection with You above all else. Grant me the wisdom and strength to acknowledge that nothing is worth jeopardizing my relationship with You. Please show me how to navigate oppressive environments and unnecessary hardships, guiding me toward freedom and liberation. Please help me understand that your plan for my life far exceeds any temporary struggles I may face. Thank You, Lord, for the promise in Psalm 32, assuring me that You will lead me along the most suitable path for my life. I am grateful for Your constant presence, guidance, and unwavering love. Help me trust Your plan and lean on Your understanding in all situations.

Affirmation

God is renewing my strength and endurance to keep going.

Personalized Prayer and Reflection: [Your personalized prayer and reflection here]

_____

_____

_____

_____

_____

_____

_____

_____

_____

_____

_____

_____

_____

_____

_____

_____

_____

_____

_____

_____

_____

_____

_____

_____

_____

_____

_____

WEEK 1- DAY 3

Egypt Unveiled:
"Unraveling the Cost of Your Stay"

*"Then you will know that I am the LORD your God, who
brought you out from under the yoke of the Egyptians."*
Exodus 6:7

**What is the cost of staying in your Egypt? (peace, health, career,
family, etc.)**

_____

_____

_____

In the heart of Egypt, the Israelites forged their existence across centuries. Though surrounded by the grandeur of their surroundings, an unseen weight bore down upon them. Despite the outward appearance of prosperity, the children of Israel toiled relentlessly, their dreams of a brighter future fading with each passing day. However, amidst this struggle, a spark of resilience remained—a steadfast yearning for freedom echoing through the ages. This echoed within the confines of My-Egypt, where the toll of enduring laborious tasks was tangible. The flickering lights and outdated infrastructure served as a testament to the monotony of daily life. Despite the challenges, many found solace in the familiarity of routine, like an old friend with whom one was hesitant to part ways. The cautionary tales of those who ventured beyond the known boundaries lingered, instilling doubt in the hearts of those contemplating change. Personally, my desire to break free was tempered by the practical concerns for my children's financial stability. Striving to justify my decision to remain, I was confronted with the realization of stagnation. Five years had passed without any progression—no resume updates or job interviews. My Egypt, flawed though it may have been, had become a sanctuary I clung to, even as the fervent cry of my heart urged me to depart. Financial constraints and logistical uncertainties only served to complicate matters further, casting doubt upon the feasibility of departure. However, amidst the turmoil, signs of transformation loomed overhead. The influx of fresh faces and promises of revitalization clashed with the reality of stagnant wages and a turbulent work environment. It became increasingly apparent that the normalization of mediocrity had clouded my judgment, blurring the distinction between complacency and determination. In moments of introspection, I pondered the deeper significance of my predicament. Could these trials have been a divine intervention, nudging me towards personal and professional growth? This newfound awareness sparked a profound internal conflict, demanding a thorough reevaluation of my circumstances and aspirations. Standing at the crossroads of familiarity and uncertainty, I knew that the journey ahead would not be easy—but perhaps, in embracing the unknown, I would find the freedom I had so long yearned to have.

Soul Search

Take a moment to assess the cost of staying in your own Egypt. Are you clinging to the familiarity of routine, hesitant to venture beyond the known boundaries? Are you sacrificing personal and professional growth in favor of stability and security? Ultimately, the decision to stay or depart lies within your hands. Nevertheless, as you weigh the costs and benefits of each path, remember that true freedom often requires the courage to embrace the unknown.

Guided Prayer

I come before You with a heart filled with gratitude for Your constant presence and guidance in my life. Just as You led the Israelites out of Egypt, you have lifted the burdens of my past and shown me the way forward. Today, I seek Your divine wisdom as I navigate my choices. Please grant me the discernment to understand the paths that lie ahead. Please help me to see the immediate consequences and the long-term effects of each decision I make. Give me clarity and purpose as I choose my direction. In Your infinite wisdom, give me the courage to let go of anything that holds me back from fulfilling Your purpose for my life. Strengthen me to overcome obstacles and challenges, knowing that Your plans for me are good. I trust in Your guidance, Lord, knowing that Your understanding surpasses mine. May Your wisdom lead me and my faith in Your providence be unwavering. I surrender my decisions and desires to You, knowing You will lead me on your chosen path. In Jesus' name

Affirmation

I hear your voice, Lord, leading me onto the path of success.

Personalized Prayer and Reflection: [Your personalized prayer and reflection here]

_____

_____

_____

_____

_____

_____

_____

_____

_____

_____

_____

_____

_____

_____

_____

_____

_____

_____

_____

_____

_____

_____

_____

_____

_____

_____

_____

_____

_____

WEEK 1- DAY 4

Crossroads of Choice: "Stay or Go - Unveiling Your Path Forward"

"Leave us alone; let us serve the Egyptian."
Exodus 14:12

What Have You Decided? Stay or Go

The saga continues as the children of Israel find themselves engulfed in the turmoil initiated by the new Pharaoh's reign. With each passing day, their once peaceful existence morphs into a harsh reality of oppression and cruelty. The Pharaoh's disregard for their contributions and significance plunges them into a state of uncertainty and fear. As the Israelites endure the weight of unbearable hardships, their longing for the comforts of Egypt intensifies. The memory of its flavorsome delicacies, the alluring taste of fish, leeks, cucumbers, and sweet onions, and the familiarity of its landscapes cast a shadow over their resolve to break free. However, beneath this longing lies a growing desire for freedom, fueled by the injustices they face. As the Israelites struggle, empathy wells within me, drawing parallels to my challenges in parting with my metaphorical Egypt. The sleepless nights, exhausting days, and countless sacrifices made for a better future intertwine with the profound attachment to familiarity. Much like the Israelites, I grapple with abandoning comfort and familiarity. Bitter tears flow because of their enslavement, their groans and cries echoing through the air, impossible to ignore. Each tear carries the weight of despair, spirits crushed by the brutality of their oppressors. In the depths of anguish, their belief in God's promise of deliverance wavers, obscured by the shadows of suffering. Facing a daunting choice in their quest for freedom, the Israelites must leave behind memories of grandeur in Egypt, a land they called home despite bitter bondage. I, too, yearn for transformation, resonating with the hesitant children of Israel. The universal theme is the struggle to let go of the familiar and confront uncertainty. My own Egypt symbolizes comfort and security but hinders my true potential. Much like the Israelites, I wrestle with the tension between clinging to the safety of what I possess and embracing the boundless opportunities that lie beyond.

Soul Search

The choice is ours: Will we stay, clinging to our fears despite their limitations and constraints? Or will we heed the call of our inner yearning for freedom, embracing the uncertainty of the journey ahead? Whether we choose to stay or leave, may we find the strength to honor our truth and follow the path that leads us closer to fulfilling our deepest desires."

Guided Prayer

Lord, I come before you, burdened by a decision that weighs heavily on my heart. I acknowledge my human limitations and seek Your divine guidance. You, who see and understand all, I ask for Your light to illuminate the path ahead of me. Grant me the wisdom to discern between right and wrong and the choices that align with Your will. Help me to set aside my desires and fears and, instead, allow Your voice to be the compass that guides my steps. Lord, if my decision does not align with Your perfect plan, I ask for Your intervention. Close the doors that should remain shut and open the ones that lead to Your intended blessings. Grant me a deep sense of peace when I walk in Your will, and let me feel uneasy when straying from Your path. I trust in Your promise that You work all things for the good of those who love You. I surrender my doubts, worries, and uncertainties into Your capable hands.

Give me the courage to let go of any wrong decision and the strength to embrace the better path You reveal. In the name of Your Son, Jesus Christ

Affirmation

I heed the voice of God, guiding my path.

Personalized Prayer and Reflection: [Your personalized prayer and reflection here]

_____

_____

_____

_____

_____

_____

_____

_____

_____

_____

_____

WEEK 1- DAY 5

Extending the Stay: "When Fear Takes the Upper Hand"

"Do not be afraid. God has come to test you so that the fear of God will be with you to keep you from sinning."
Exodus 20:20

What are you afraid of?

_____

_____

_____

Fear carries a peculiar power in the hidden corners of our minds, ensnaring us into terrifying places long after reason dictates that we flee. It threads its way through the fabric of our lives, dragging us deeper into darkness and ensnaring us in the grip of discomfort and despair. Reflecting on the initial encounter between Moses, Aaron, and the Israelites, one can sense the palpable hope and anticipation that filled the air. The miraculous signs and wonders performed by God left the Israelites in awe, fueling their aspirations for freedom and a brighter future. However, perhaps they overlooked Aaron's cautionary words, warning of the demanding journey ahead. In this parallel, I resonate with my experiences—the anticipation of deliverance, the yearning for better days, and the biting fear of further hardships and disappointments. For years, I clung to the belief that relentless hard work and determination were the keys to success. I poured countless hours into my professional endeavors to prove my worth and earn recognition. However, with each passing day, my efforts seemed to be met with ever-increasing demands and diminishing acknowledgment. The ongoing pursuit of validation from my superiors only worsened my disillusionment. During introspection, I was drawn to a peculiar sight—a faded wreath decorating the office door. Its weathered appearance hinted at a history of commemorating departed colleagues, stirring within me a mixture of emotions—anger, frustration, and a profound sense of disregard. It was as if my years of dedication and accomplishments had been rendered worthless, even in death. These sentiments gradually evolved into a pervasive sense of entitlement, simmering beneath the surface for years. As I contemplated resigning from my job, this entitlement manifested as a reluctance to let go—I felt deserving of more. Stepping away from my position felt like a daunting leap into the unknown, fraught with uncertainty. The anxieties that plagued me echoed the uncertainties of the Israelites in the desert— what lay ahead? How would I provide for my family? It was a bitter pill to swallow, contemplating that all my efforts and sacrifices might have been in vain. Within this turmoil, a sobering realization dawned upon me—much like Pharaoh's disregard for Joseph's contributions, I had become a casualty of a system that failed to recognize genuine dedication. My labor seemed only to invite greater demands while recognition dwindled—a parallel to the plight of the Israelites under Pharaoh's rule. Yet, despite this hesitance to leave, a nagging question persisted: what was I terrified of?

Soul Search

What fears hold you back from embracing change and pursuing the path to fulfillment? Is it the fear of the unknown, of stepping into uncharted territory where outcomes are uncertain? Alternatively, perhaps it is the fear of failure, not living up to expectations, or falling short of your aspirations. Maybe the fear of leaving behind the familiar, the comfort of routines and relationships, has become ingrained in your life. Or is it the fear of judgment, of what others might think or say if you were to veer off the expected course?

Nevertheless, what if we were to confront these fears head-on? What if we acknowledge their presence yet refuse to let them dictate our choices? What if we were to embrace change not as a threat but as an opportunity for growth and self-discovery?

Guided Prayer

Lord, I come before you, seeking your strength and courage to break free from the grip of fear that has held me captive for too long. You are the ultimate source of power and light, and I turn to you in my time of need. I confess my apprehensions and anxieties to you, knowing that you understand the depths of my heart. Grant me your divine guidance to navigate through this challenging situation and emerge victorious on the other side. Help me discern when to step forward, even when the path seems unclear and daunting. It fills me with the courage to confront my fears head-on, knowing that I am never alone with you by my side. Please open my eyes to the opportunities beyond this place of discomfort and despair. Strengthen my faith and trust in your divine plan, knowing you have a purpose for every trial I face. Lord, grant me the wisdom, clarity, and resolve to overcome fear and walk boldly into the future you have prepared for me, in Jesus' Name.

Affirmation

"I am strong and courageous, breaking free from fear with faith and grace."

Personalized Prayer and Reflection: [Your personalized prayer and reflection here]

WEEK 1- DAY 6

Embracing the Horizon: "Finally, Ready to Go"

"At the end of the 430 years, to the very day,
all the Lord's divisions left Egypt."
Exodus 12:41

Are You Ready Yet?

_____

_____

_____

Getting out of a challenging situation was way more complex than I thought. Back then, I used to judge people who wanted to end a relationship but could not. I figured they were just too weak or too attached. However, when facing the same challenge, I realized I was not exactly thrilled with my situation, and I did not lack determination. Instead, I was dealing with this overwhelming fear that overshadowed everything else. In the middle of that struggle, something unexpected happened. It was not part of my plan, but I started praying, fasting, and sending out tons of job applications – like trying to find my way through a maze of uncertainty. And then, on top of it all, I thought maybe this was all God's plan. However, His silence was deafening, like a never-ending drought in my Egypt. The sound of unanswered prayers seemed to go on forever, leaving me wondering about God's timing. No matter how hard I prayed, nothing seemed to change.

I knew God could do anything, but I was still stuck in the exact old job search. To make things worse, I started worrying that trying to do things God's way might take longer. It felt like I was expecting a miracle to happen in the blink of an eye, but all I was getting were obstacles and setbacks. And then I thought about the story of the Israelites in Exodus. They were promised freedom from slavery, but every step forward seemed to come with new problems. They could not catch a break, with Pharaoh making things worse at every turn. They begged God for help, just like I was doing then, but it felt like help was miles away. God sent Moses and Aaron to help them, but they even got into trouble with the Pharaoh. The guy was so stubborn that he would not listen to anything they said.

Furthermore, doubt started creeping in as they waited for God to come through, just like it was for me. Going through all that made me realize something strange: I felt more comfortable working hard for what I needed, only turning to God as a last resort – like asking your parents for help only when you are desperate. However, over time, I saw that God helps those who help themselves. I was ready to take matters into my own hands, but it felt like God was not on the same page. I wanted to trust that God would provide for me, but waiting for His response wore out. It was tempting to return to my old ways and stick with what I knew, even if it was not the best option. My journey felt like the Israelites' struggle: waiting on God, trying to keep the faith, and dealing with setback after setback. It was a rollercoaster of emotions, but it also made me think about the bigger picture. Maybe there was more to that waiting game than I could see. Maybe there was a bigger plan at work, even if I could not see it yet."

Soul Search

Just as the Israelites grappled with leaving behind the familiarity of Egypt for the promise of freedom, you, too, stand at a pivotal moment of decision. Are you willing to embrace change to confront the unknown with courage and determination? So, I ask you again: after all you have learned, are you ready to take that step out of Egypt to embark on the path of transformation and possibility?

Guided Prayer

Lord, as I faced adversity, I asked for wisdom to see challenges as opportunities for growth and setbacks as mere steppingstones on my journey toward my aspirations. With your guidance, I navigated life's twists and turns with grace and perseverance. I drew strength from the wellspring of faith within me, rising above limitations and overcoming hurdles. Your wisdom guided my actions, and I filled my heart with unwavering belief that I could surmount any difficulty. In your name, I prayed for the strength to navigate life's trials with steadfast faith.

Affirmation

I confidently forge ahead, embracing challenges as steppingstones to my success.

Personalized Prayer and Reflection: [Your personalized prayer and reflection here]

_____

_____

_____

_____

_____

WEEK 1- DAY 7

Setting Spiritual Goals and Intentions

Reflection: As you conclude the initial seven days of devotion, take a moment to look ahead. Your spiritual journey is an ongoing adventure; setting clear intentions can guide your path. Today, let us explore how to set meaningful goals and preferences for the coming weeks and months.

"Commit to the LORD whatever you do,
and he will establish your plans."
Proverbs 16:3

Reflect on Your Journey: Take a few moments to reflect on the insights and experiences you have gained during the past week. What lessons have you learned? What aspects of your spirituality have been most meaningful to you?

_____

_____

_____

_____

_____

_____

Identify Areas for Growth: Reflect on the aspects of your spiritual life you wish to enhance. This reflection may include your connection with God, your inner peace, your compassion for others, or any other aspect that holds significance for you.

_____

_____

_____

_____

_____

Create a Timeline: Assign timelines to your goals. When do you hope to achieve them? Setting deadlines can provide motivation and structure to your spiritual journey.

_____

_____

_____

_____

_____

Write a Personal Declaration: Craft a personal declaration or affirmation summarizing your intentions. Use positive and empowering language that resonates with you.

_____

_____

_____

_____

_____

WEEK 2- DAY 8

Turning Disappointment into Determination: "Navigating Life's Unexpected Twists"

"If only we had died by the Lord's hand in Egypt."
Exodus 16:3

Are you setting yourself up for disappointment?

_____

_____

_____

In an unexpected turn of events, I engaged in a candid conversation with my colleague S'harr, which added a unique twist to our friendship. As we spoke, she expressed her gratitude for my inspiring her to step away from her nearly two-decade-long career and embark on a fresh journey. Her transition into this new path appeared almost effortless, stirring a mixture of emotions within me. Listening intently to S'harr's words of encouragement, I could not help but feel a surge of conflicting emotions: envy, disappointment, anger, and a sense of entitlement. Behind a wry smile, I concealed the turmoil, questioning her understanding of the challenges ahead.

Had she truly experienced hardship? Had she faced unemployment and struggled to meet financial obligations like mine? These thoughts raced through my mind as I tried to make sense of her seemingly charmed journey. What added to my bewilderment was the realization that S'harr did not adhere to the Christian faith as I did. It seemed improbable that she had sought divine guidance or offered prayers for her new endeavor. However, she spoke of securing her new job without applying, which heightened my excitement and perplexity. Her stories of others landing jobs almost magically fueled my curiosity, prompting me to question whether some divine hand had overlooked my struggles. This sensation of abandonment evoked memories of the ancient Israelites, who must have pondered if their God had forsaken them during their trials in Egypt. I could not shake the parallel between my feelings and those of the ancient Israelites. Just as they may have felt disappointed and let down by God during their time of hardship, I grappled with similar emotions. The Israelites, enslaved in Egypt, cried out to their God for deliverance, only to endure years of suffering and uncertainty. Their journey from slavery to freedom was fraught with challenges, and at times, it must have seemed as if their prayers were brushed aside. In the same vein, as I reflected on my struggles and the seeming ease of S'harr's transition, I could not help but wonder if there was a divine plan at play, one that I struggled to comprehend. Did God favor others while leaving some of us to toil in obscurity? Were my prayers unheard, my pleas unanswered? Like the Israelites wandering in the desert, I felt adrift, searching for meaning during hardship and disappointment. With these thoughts swirling in my mind, I could not help but wonder if my struggles were part of a larger narrative where adversity catalyzed growth and transformation. Maybe, just maybe, S'harr's journey was a reminder that there was a plan for each of us that unfolded in unexpected ways, challenging us to embrace uncertainty.

Searching for Gratitude

Even in the face of setbacks or challenges, valuable lessons can be learned, new perspectives can be gained, and unexpected blessings can be found. By opening our hearts and minds to the possibility of gratitude, we invite positivity and light into our lives, even in the darkest times. So, let us pause and reflect: is there any reason to be thankful in these situations? Let us explore together and discover the gifts of gratitude waiting to be uncovered.

Guided Prayer

Lord, I come before you, acknowledging the presence of entitlement within me that has led to disappointment and unrest. I ask for your divine guidance in cleansing me of this spirit and leading me toward a path of humility and gratitude. In your infinite wisdom, help me release the grip of entitlement I hold towards my fellow human beings and the flawed systems of this world. Remind me, O Lord, that every good and perfect gift comes from you and that your provisions are abundant and timely. I repent for my prideful demands upon you and others, which stem from a sense of unwarranted entitlement. Please grant me the strength to overcome this weakness, replacing it with unwavering trust in your providence. As I immerse myself in the richness of your holy scriptures, may I find solace in the assurance that you hear my prayers and answer them according to your plan.

Let my obedience to faithfully follow your path remedy my misguided expectations that lie outside the boundaries of your blessings. I surrender my heart, desires, and aspirations to your perfect will. Mold me into a vessel of humility, contentment, and gratitude.

As I seek to walk in step with your divine purpose, may I be liberated from the chains of entitlement and, instead, become a channel of your grace, compassion, and love to those around me.

Affirmation

I will accept God's unchanging love, even when my desires go unmet.

Personalized Prayer and Reflection: [Your personalized prayer and reflection here]

_____

_____

_____

_____

_____

_____

_____

_____

_____

_____

_____

_____

_____

Stuck in Neutral: "Navigating Life's Puzzles in the Waiting Lane"

"Then Pharaoh will think, 'The Israelites are confused.
They are trapped in the wilderness!"
Exodus 14: 3

Are You Stuck in your decision?

_____

_____

_____

_____

In life's journey, we often encounter moments where the burden of decision-making feels overwhelming. It is akin to standing at a crossroads, unsure of which path to tread, held back by the fear of making a misstep. This sensation of being ensnared in indecision can be exasperating and disheartening, leaving us adrift and uncertain about moving forward. For someone like me, who typically possesses clarity in decision-making for desired outcomes, experiencing indecision was a novel challenge. However, there I was, metaphorically stuck in my tracks, driving down a steep incline only to find my progress halted as my vehicle refused to ascend the next slope. Despite my efforts to rev the engine, it felt as though an invisible force had arrested my momentum. The stark reality that this was no dream made the situation even more surreal. I was genuinely trapped in my car, unable to move forward, with no clear solution. Confusion clouded my mind as I desperately attempted to kickstart the stalled engine. Panic began to take hold as I grappled with the gravity of the predicament. Then, a sudden epiphany dawned on me: I had been coasting down the hill in neutral, leaving my car ill-equipped to tackle the upcoming ascent. The remedy was simple yet elusive—I needed to shift gears into drive. It was a straightforward solution that had eluded me in the heat of the moment. As I sat there contemplating my next move, the specter of my past loomed large. The attraction of returning to my old job, my personal "Egypt," was strong.

Deep down, I knew that succumbing to this allure would only prolong my indecision, trapping me in a cycle of stagnation and missed opportunities. Reflecting on the Israelites enduring centuries of slavery, I pondered their seemingly futile hope for deliverance. Doubt plagued their hearts, even as Moses, the hope-bearer, questioned his influence. Imagine the Israelites toiling under the sun, their spirits crushed by oppression, and each day blurred into the next, their hopes for freedom dwindling as they remained ensnared in Pharaoh's tyranny. Despite their fervent prayers and pleas for deliverance, their cries seemed to fall on deaf ears, leaving them mired in despair. In my parallel struggle, after years of pleading with God for transformation, disillusionment began to creep over me. I wondered when justice would prevail and the cycle of destructive behaviors would end. The idea of leaving behind the familiar held no appeal. My friend Flo's unconventional advice to let go faced strong opposition within my stubborn heart. However, her words carried an undeniable truth: when God signals you to move, it is essential to respond swiftly. Despite this, I was veiled in rebellion, indifferent to the prospect of ultimate deliverance or positivity.

Interestingly, God foresaw my reluctance, just as He anticipated Pharaoh's skepticism about the Israelites. "Pharaoh visualized the Israelites wandering in a foreign land, lost in dire confusion; he imagined the parched wilderness would trap them. "Similarly, I imagined "My Egypt" mocking my predicament, scoffing, "Lorraine aimlessly roams, adrift and bewildered; her choices have confined her." That moment served as a metaphor for the more significant struggles in my life. Like the ancient Israelites, who wandered in the desert for forty years, I felt lost and directionless, trapped in a cycle of uncertainty and doubt. They longed for freedom from their bondage but hesitated to embrace the unknown path. In my resistance, I failed to see the wisdom in Flo's words and God's call. My rebellion kept me imprisoned, blind to the possibility of a brighter future. Despite the echoing doubts and the allure of familiarity, I knew deep down that I needed to break free from indecision's shackles. Each day felt like a struggle against my doubts and fears. However, amidst the turmoil, a glimmer of hope flickered—a reminder that there is potential for transformation even in the darkest times. So, with each passing day, I strive to heed the call to action, shift from neutrality, and embrace the journey towards a new beginning.

Searching for Gratitude

As we navigate the uncertainties and complexities of life's crossroads, let us not lose sight of the blessings surrounding us. Despite the fog of indecision, there are still rays of light to be found, moments of beauty to be appreciated, and reasons to be thankful. Let us persevere in our quest for gratitude, even when the path ahead seems unclear. Let us cultivate a spirit of thankfulness that transcends our circumstances, guiding us through the uncertainties and illuminating our way forward. Together, let us embrace the journey of seeking gratitude, finding joy, and discovering the treasures of appreciation.

Guided prayer

Lord, I come before You, acknowledging the countless times You have graciously come to my aid. May the radiant memories of Your past interventions light my way, leading me to release my grip on 'My Egypt.' I surrender my needs and insecurities into Your capable hands, trusting Your divine plan. Lord, help me to stand on Your promises, knowing Your provision surpasses any resources that 'My Egypt' may offer. If You have called me to forsake it, I am steadfast in my conviction that Your blessings far exceed its grasp. In this moment of surrender, I recognize that Your purpose transcends my comprehension. With unwavering faith, I place myself entirely in Your care, knowing that Your ability to provide goes beyond the boundaries of my perception. As You have done in the past, I am confident that You will lead me through this new chapter, illuminating a path far beyond my current sight.

Affirmation

I am free from neutrality's grip, releasing all resistance. My future awaits, and I embrace it with open arms.

Personalized Prayer and Reflection: [Your personalized prayer and reflection here]

_____

_____

_____

_____

_____

_____

WEEK 2- DAY 10

Stepping into Freedom: My Passover Journey Begins

"On that very day, the Lord brought the Israelites out of Egypt."
Exodus 12:51

What does true freedom mean to you?

_____

_____

_____

Counting down the last month in My-Egypt, I was ready to go. I had stopped receiving calls and seeing patients, prepared for everything to end, including this farewell party. The farewell gathering, a tradition in My Egypt marking the end of a significant chapter, carried a blend of bitter and sweet emotions. Colleagues, acquaintances, and well-wishers filled the room, creating an atmosphere filled with laughter, chatter, and heartfelt embraces. However, amidst the warmth, a subtle insincerity occasionally tainted the occasion. Some attendees were present out of obligation or curiosity rather than a genuine connection. Although polite, conversations lacked depth, serving as a prelude to heartfelt goodbyes lacking in authenticity. Amid the well-wishing and clinking glasses, I longed to curate the guest list, inviting those who had been part of my journey. This desire stemmed from a deep longing for a more intimate gathering, a chance to celebrate with those whose connections ran deep and whose well-wishes were genuinely sincere. In my ideal scenario, I envisioned handpicking attendees, creating an environment where farewells were more than superficial gestures. This imagined gathering would embody a genuine exchange of sentiments, stories, and laughter, reflecting the shared experiences and cherished moments that had shaped our journey to that very point.

Truthfully, the event felt hurried, everything moving at a fast pace. The feeling of being rushed was unsettling, leaving little room for error. This sense of haste was not new to me; I was always the slowest eater in my family due to my picky eating habits. Despite unwelcome comments and pressure to hurry up, I savored each bite, finding solace in taking my time, even eating. For the children of Israel, this cry to hurry came from God himself. God gave them unusual instructions about eating that would make every mom cringe: devour your meal and dress swiftly for travel with sandals on your feet and a walking stick in your hand. The urgency in God's instructions to the children of Israel resonated with my desire to savor life's moments. On that momentous Passover night in Egypt, anticipation and a sense of impending change hung heavy. Excitement and fear mingled, for the Israelites were about to witness a divine intervention of epic proportions. Outside, oblivious to the supernatural forces, modern Egyptians continued their evening routines. Little did they know that the God of Israel was gearing up to bring judgment upon the false gods of Egypt and punish Pharaoh for his cruelty towards the Israelites. The Passover meal, typically a time of familial bonding and celebration, took on a different tone that night. It was a meal eaten in haste, a reminder of the urgency of their departure. The taste of unleavened bread and bitter herbs lingered on their tongues, symbolizing the bitterness of their enslavement and the swift exit that awaited them. In my rush and chaos, I found inspiration in the details of that ancient Passover night. The urgency, the divine protection, and the eventual triumph became a beacon of hope. Much like the Israelites, I, too, faced my challenges and uncertainties, but the story of that night served as a reminder that even in the darkest hours, divine intervention and freedom are possible.

Searching for Gratitude

Let us pause momentarily and reflect on the blessings surrounding us, even amidst the fog of confusion. Perhaps it is the warmth of a loved one's embrace, the beauty of nature unfolding outside our window, or the simple pleasures of a quiet moment alone. As we navigate the unknown, let us cultivate a spirit of thankfulness that transcends our circumstances. Let us train our eyes to see the silver linings, the small victories, and the moments of grace that pepper our days.

Guided Prayer

Lord, I come before you with a heart full of gratitude and a soul longing for freedom. I recognize that true freedom begins within, in the depths of my being, where your divine presence resides. I surrender my fears, doubts, and limitations to you, dear God. Release me from the chains of self-doubt and insecurity. Please grant me the strength to let go of the past and embrace the lessons it taught me without letting it define my future. Guide my steps as I walk the path to freedom. Please help me forgive others and myself for the mistakes and hurts of the past. Grant me the wisdom to learn from my experiences, the courage to face my challenges, and the grace to accept the things I cannot change. Empower me to control my thoughts, actions, and reactions so I may create a life of purpose and fulfillment.

Affirmation

"Fearless, I step forward with courage."

Personalized Prayer and Reflection: [Your personalized prayer and reflection here]

Lorraine Murray-Richardson

WEEK 2- DAY 11

Breaking Chains: Avoiding Self-Sabotage During Your Passover Journey"

"The Lord replied, 'I will personally go with you, Moses, and I will give you rest—everything will be fine for you.'"
Exodus 33:14 NLT

How are your fears and insecurities influencing your decisions and actions?

_____

_____

_____

The excitement and hope of that night when God led the children of Israel out of Egypt had gradually transformed into a treacherous journey marred by doubt and fear. The words, 'It would have been better for us to serve the Egyptians than to die in the desert!' echoed like a mournful hymn across the barren landscape, the anguished cry of a people on the brink of surrender. These words, heavy with the weight of desperation, condensed the sentiments that now gripped the hearts of the Israelites. The fear of the unknown had seeped into their souls, eroding their resolve and clouding their vision of the future. The promise of freedom, once a beacon illuminating their path, now seemed like a distant memory, obscured by the looming shadows of doubt. I am familiar with these words of surrender and the desire to turn back to the captivity I had fled. Confronted with a daunting truth, I was on the verge of sabotaging my future. The reluctance that permeated my spirit threatened to shackle me into the chains of the past, preventing me from embracing the destiny I had longed for all this time. An eerie dream shrouded me, reaffirming that change was stirring within the depths of my being. The urgency to depart from 'My Egypt' was undeniable, yet I found myself standing unprepared at the daunting crossroads of transformation. In the realm of dreams, I stood within a birthing room, caught in the throes of the second stage of labor – a fully dilated cervix and the imminent arrival of a newborn. The baby waited in the birth canal, a potent symbol of the next step I had to take. However, my dream took an unexpected turn. While physically prepared for this transformative moment, my mental and emotional state raised concerns. Strangely, I had resolved to delay the birth, resisting the inevitable. Having experienced childbirth before, I understood the risks of a baby lodged in the birth canal. The urge to push became overwhelming as pressure mounted on the pelvic nerves. In my dream, physicians and nurses implored me to yield to the birthing process, but my response was an emphatic 'NO!' – a declaration of resistance, a staunch stance against succumbing to the momentum of change. The echoes of that dream lingered, refusing to dissolve. It served as a wake-up call, highlighting my subconscious self-sabotage – a realization that I was jeopardizing everything, from my physical health to my overall well-being. Departing from 'My Egypt' was an undeniable imperative, although it was not my initial preference. Long ago, I had silently vowed never to leave before my destined time. I faced a struggle like the Children of Israel – torn between embracing change and holding onto the familiar. Like them, I had to let go of what I knew for the unknown. I learned that embracing growth meant letting go of resistance, even when it did not happen on my terms.

Searching for Gratitude

Life has a way of throwing us curveballs. In those moments of difficulty and uncertainty, it is easy to let negativity take hold and overshadow the blessings that surround us. But what if I told you there is always something to be grateful for, even in the most challenging times? Look for opportunities to cultivate gratitude in every aspect of your life – in your relationships, work, health, and even the challenges you face, for it is often in the darkest moments that the light of gratitude shines the brightest.

Guided Prayer

Lord, I am seeking your wisdom and strength. I acknowledge my struggles and fears, especially the ones that lead me to sabotage my future. I ask for your guidance and support as I navigate the path ahead. I confess my human frailties before you. I recognize the patterns within me that hold me back, the self-doubt and fear that prevent me from reaching my full potential. I lay these struggles bare before you, acknowledging that only with your guidance can I overcome them. Help me release the doubts and resistance that hold me back. Please grant me the clarity to recognize my self-sabotaging tendencies and the courage to overcome them. Fill my heart with determination and faith so I may embrace the opportunities you provide without hesitation or fear. I surrender my worries and insecurities to you, trusting that you have a plan for my future.

Please grant me the wisdom to make choices that align with your divine purpose for my life. Strengthen my resolve to let go of the past and confidently move forward. Please grant me the strength to let go of the doubts that cloud my mind and the resistance that hampers my progress. Help me break free from my insecurities, allowing me to step into the fullness of my potential. Empower me to silence the inner critic, replacing self-doubt with self-assurance. Please grant me the clarity to recognize my self-sabotaging tendencies and the courage to overcome them. Fill my heart with determination and faith so I may embrace the opportunities you provide without hesitation or fear.

Affirmation

"I surrender my self-sabotaging tendencies to the Almighty, embracing the strength within me."

Personalized Prayer and Reflection: [Your personalized prayer and reflection here]

_____

_____

_____

_____

_____

_____

_____

_____

_____

_____

_____

_____

_____

Signs of Certainty: "Navigating the Path to Your Purpose!"

"The Lord replied, 'I will personally go with you, Moses, and I will give you rest—everything will be fine for you.'"
Exodus 33:14

"How do you find solace in believing every trial and joy in your life is part of a greater purpose?

_____

_____

_____

Pharaoh, a perplexing figure, remains a steadfast opponent despite the unrelenting barrage of nine devastating plagues. It began with the waters of the Nile River turning to blood, the lifeblood of Egypt tainted, fouling the once-refreshing source of sustenance. The people were horrified, but Pharaoh remained resolute, his pride closing his eyes to the suffering of his people. Despite the pleas of the people, Pharaoh stood firm, refusing to release the Israelites from their bondage, his resolve unshaken. Then came the frogs, an army of amphibians invading homes, croaking their deafening chorus and leaving no corner untouched. Even as the people implored Pharaoh to relent, he remained unmoved by their appeals.

Next, the dust of the land transformed into swarms of gnats, a relentless cloud of tiny creatures that filled the air, causing misery and discomfort wherever they went. The once-bountiful fields now withered under this pestilence, but Pharaoh's obstinacy only hardened, his heart frozen against mercy. Flies descended upon Egypt, following the gnats in a thick, buzzing cloud. These relentless insects tormented livestock and people alike, yet Pharaoh's resolve remained unshaken. Pharaoh's obstinacy only hardened as the stench of suffering permeated the air, his heart frozen against mercy.

Then came the boils, painful sores that afflicted man and beast, leaving the once-proud Egyptians humbled and desperate for relief. Even Pharaoh's advisors, confronted with the devastation, implored him to free the Israelites. Yet, he remained unmoved by their appeals. A hailstorm of unprecedented fury followed, destroying crops and property and bringing famine and despair to the land. Pharaoh's heart softened momentarily at each plague, leading him to beg Moses for relief. Locusts came; next, a swarm of locusts descended, a dark cloud devouring every trace of green in their path. Egypt lay in ruins, its people on the brink of despair, yet still, Pharaoh clung to his pride, unwilling to release the enslaved Israelites. Finally, darkness descended upon Egypt, a thick, impenetrable darkness that enveloped the land for three long days. The people huddled in fear, gripped by the terror of the unknown, but even as the darkness loomed, Pharaoh's heart remained veiled in its own shadow. These plagues, unleashed by Pharaoh's hand, brought Egypt to its knees. The land and its people suffered each time, yet his resistance persisted. He clung to the hope of delivering the final blow to the Children of Israel, a blow from which they would never recover. I imagine his advisors beseeching him to relent, urging him to release the Israelites. Yet, his heart remained hardened, a testament to the stubbornness of power. Pharaoh's heart temporarily softened with each plague, compelling him to plead with Moses to intercede. He made promises to free the people, only to retract his words once the affliction subsided, subjecting the Israelites to ongoing torment. However, the final plague was unlike the others.

God would not allow Pharaoh to seize the initiative this time. Exodus 12:12 captures the poignant moment at midnight when wailing echoed through the Egyptian households as God visited judgment upon them. It was a turning point, a shift in the tides of fate, as the narrative unfolded with divine precision. Perhaps I should have marked my own Passover at midnight, a subtle choice to avoid the smirks and hidden joys that marred the grand celebration of my existence. I saw the smirk on Bellena's face; that is what we call her, Nosy Bellena, to be exact. She was a pain, an actual problematic employee, leaving almost an impression that she had won. However, deep within, I knew better; I found comfort in knowing that A divine plan guided my journey. The hours ticked by slowly, the wait until 4:30 a Herculean feat, and as my Passover (my farewell) concluded, a mixture of gratitude and reflection settled upon me. Lord, I am thankful for the resounding praises that have filled the air, the affirmations of my work and character. I am grateful that You struck first, imprinting a memory of my name as one associated with good rather than evil. Though my plan may appear absent on the surface, it is clear to me – You are my plan, my unwavering compass guiding me forward.

Searching for Gratitude

Gratitude is not merely a practice of tallying our blessings; it extends far beyond that. It is about delving deep into the fabric of our experiences and extracting meaning and purpose from every moment, regardless of its difficulty or pain. It is about recognizing that invaluable lessons await discovery, even in life's most challenging chapters. When we embrace gratitude, we open ourselves to the wisdom that adversity brings. We learn to find strength in our vulnerabilities, rise above our circumstances, and navigate life's twists and turns with resilience and courage. Every setback becomes an opportunity for growth, every obstacle a stepping stone on our journey toward self-discovery

Guided Prayer

Lord, in life's uncertainties, I come to You with a heart full of gratitude for the certainty You provide. In Your infinite wisdom, you have woven a purpose into the very fabric of my being. I find solace in the assurance that my existence is not a mere accident but a deliberate creation with a profound purpose. Grant me the strength to embrace the certainty of Your plan, even when the path ahead seems shrouded in shadows. Help me to trust in the purpose You have designed for me, understanding that every twist and turn, every joy and sorrow, is a part of Your divine masterpiece. May I find purpose in every moment, recognizing that even minor acts can serve a greater good. Help me to live with intention, to be mindful of the impact I have on the world around me, and to align my actions with Your divine purpose.

Affirmation

I am confident in my purpose and sure of my path. With unwavering faith, I trust in the divine plan guiding me forward.

Personalized Prayer and Reflection: [Your personalized prayer and reflection here]

_____

_____

_____

_____

_____

Lorraine Murray-Richardson

WEEK 2- DAY 13

Silent Victories: Embracing Divine Departures and Personal Triumphs

"And I will make the Egyptians favorably
disposed toward this people."
Exodus 3:21

How do your quiet successes, shaped by divine guidance and personal growth, reveal the strength within you and the impact of faith on your journey?

_____

_____

_____

I find myself strangely captivated by the image of the Israelites defiantly marching out of Egypt, their heads held high and hands raised triumphantly. Not only were they carrying their personal belongings, but also the precious coffin containing Joseph's dry bones. This sight fills me with a sense of awe and wonder. The very same Egyptians who had once heartlessly thrown Hebrew infants into the Nile and subjected the Israelites to years of brutal mistreatment were now unwitting instruments of divine providence. In a stunning twist of fate, God's favor transformed these oppressors into bearers of unimaginable wealth for the Israelites. The once-cruel Egyptians became conduits of gold, silver, and unparalleled riches, adorning the Israelites with the spoils of victory. This breathtaking scene speaks volumes about the power of divine intervention and justice. Likewise, as I sit back and recall my ritual of clocking in at work and secretly escaping to a realm of daydreams filled with the fantasy of quitting one's job, it becomes a delightful amusement familiar to many. Tales of audacious exits abound, each more amusing than the last, though my favorite remains locked away, too embarrassing to share. Like many, I have indulged in this mental escapade, envisioning my glorious departure day far too often, meticulously crafting my exit plan in conversations with my friend.

In my mind's eye, I strode away like the children of Israel, head held high, a triumphant fist raised in defiance. My friend's words fueled the fire, encouraging a playful rebellion. "Kick a few desks, throw some chairs," she suggested, igniting laughter that resonated with shared experiences of being mistreated, lied to, and taken advantage of. Our camaraderie made it all the more entertaining – two disciplined Christian women, wives, mothers, and professionals reveling in mischievous banter that once belonged to wilder days. Tempting as it was to return the playful jab, to tease her about her past exploits, I held back. Though our banter was harmless, a mere dance of words, I found solace in its nonsense. Today, I mused, would have been the perfect day to confront nosy Bellena and her cohorts, to set her straight and address the years of misleading tales she has spun. Or perhaps, to tell miserable Jhelma that her hostile demeanor had not gone unnoticed, that her fictional stories were transparent to all. These imagined confrontations held an allure, a sense of empowerment, even if it was fleeting. However, as I journeyed through these whimsical thoughts, a greater truth emerged – rooted in divine promises. In Genesis 15:14, God assured Abraham that the children of Israel would leave Egypt with great possessions. This promise resurfaced in Exodus 3:21 when God confirmed to Moses that the Israelites would not depart empty-handed. However, my reality unfolded differently. As I walked away, the rhythm of my heels clicking against the floor replaced the hushed tread of flats, silencing the familiar sound that once announced my presence. My hands hung empty at my sides, marking a silent departure that resonated with a different kind of victory – the triumph of choosing to move forward, even while carrying the weight of memories and emotions. On that day, I walked out with my good name, character, work ethic, knowledge, and more, each invaluable trait serving as a compass guiding me toward my destiny. Though devoid of tangible gold and silver, this departure was profoundly rich in its significance.

Searching for Gratitude

As we journey through life, we often strive for success in our careers, relationships, or personal endeavors. Moreover, when success does come knocking at our door, it is easy to get caught up in the whirlwind of achievement and forget to pause and give thanks for the blessings bestowed upon us. Amid our accomplishments, let us take a moment to reflect on the journey that brought us to this point—the obstacles overcome, the lessons learned, and the support of those who stood by our side. Let us celebrate the result, growth, and transformation that occurred along the way.

Guided prayer

Lord, help me to remember Your promise that I will not leave empty-handed when I place my trust in You. I surrender my fears, doubts, and uncertainties to Your loving hands. Grant me the faith to trust in Your divine plan, even when I cannot see the way forward. Help me to believe in Your promises, knowing that You are faithful in fulfilling them. I pray for Your guidance in making wise decisions and the courage to face whatever comes my way. Lord, I trust that with You by my side, I can overcome any obstacle and find fulfillment in Your purpose for my life. Fill my heart with peace, Lord, and strengthen my faith in Your unfailing love. Help me not leave empty-handed but carry the blessings of Your grace, wisdom, and provision with me on my journey. I place my life and future and trust in Your hands, Lord. Thank You for Your endless love and grace. In Jesus' name, I pray.

Affirmation

"I affirm, through the grace of God, that I will not be empty-handed. I am a magnet for His abundance, prosperity, and opportunities."

Personalized Prayer and Reflection: [Your personalized prayer and reflection here]

_____

_____

_____

_____

_____

_____

_____

_____

_____

_____

_____

_____

Lorraine Murray-Richardson

WEEK 2- DAY 14

Reflection and Gratitude.

Reflection and Gratitude: "Give thanks in all circumstances; for this is the will of God in Christ Jesus for you." - 1 Thessalonians 5:18 (ESV)

Take a moment to reflect on the blessings in your life. Consider the people, experiences, and moments that bring you joy, comfort, and inspiration. As you acknowledge these blessings, you will find that gratitude can shift your perspective and open your heart to the beauty surrounding you. Approach these prompts with deep introspection and sincerity, making your appreciation practice a profoundly personal and transformative journey. (**Choose one or do all.**)

Gratitude Challenge: For the next seven days, commit to a daily gratitude practice. Each day, write down three things you are thankful for. They can be as simple as a sunbeam streaming through your window, a kind word from a friend, or the aroma of your favorite tea. Reflect on why you are grateful for each blessing.

1. _____

_____

_____

_____

_____

2. _____
   _____
   _____
   _____
   _____

3. _____
   _____
   _____
   _____
   _____

4. _____
   _____
   _____
   _____
   _____

5. _____
   _____
   _____
   _____
   _____

6. _____

_____

_____

_____

_____

Gratitude for Lessons: Reflect on a mistake or failure that taught you an important life lesson. Write about the growth from this experience and express gratitude for the wisdom gained.

_____

_____

_____

_____

_____

Write a letter to your future expressing gratitude for the accomplishments, experiences, and relationships you hope to have. Visualize these future blessings and embrace gratitude as if they have already happened.

_____

_____

_____

_____

_____

_____

WEEK 3- DAY 15

Embracing Divine Abundance:
"Leaving 'My Egypt' with Full Hands"

"So that when you leave, you will not go empty-handed."
Exodus 3:21

How did you find the courage to leave the familiar, embrace the unknown, and face challenges with determination?

_____

_____

_____

At precisely 5:45pm, I ventured out, walking away from the walls that had contained my experiences and memories. Now eerily quiet, the halls felt oppressively suffocating, lacking the usual bustling activity. A realization struck me – for the first time, no one was bidding me a casual 'See you on Monday.' It was an unexpected pang, a stark reminder of the finality of this moment. Yet the absence of that defiant fist caught me off guard, stirring a surge of conflicting emotions within me. Just the day before, I had felt so resolute, longing to raise that fist in triumphant defiance – a gesture aimed at those who had mocked me, those who had turned a blind eye to my departure, and especially those who had transformed 'My Egypt' into an unworkable mess. Then, in a twist of whimsical fate, I realized I had deliberately left my purse at home, though the reason eluded me. Armed only with a cell phone, I entered the elevator. Those forty-four seconds felt like an eternity, a space ripe for contemplation. It dawned on me – I was leaving 'My Egypt' empty-handed. A wave of emotion washed over me, a peculiar blend of liberation and vulnerability. Standing at the exit door, a pang of disappointment gripped me, the weight of missed opportunities settling heavily on my shoulders.

Then, like a whisper in the wind, a faint voice questioned, 'Are you truly leaving empty-handed?' Was it a challenge to my conviction or a reminder of unnoticed treasures? My thoughts raced – the forsaken promotion, the relinquished raise, the security of 'My Egypt,' that haven of economic stability. Exodus 3:20-22 danced through my mind, its audacious promises now unfolding in my narrative. I marveled at the audacity of God's declaration: 'I will stretch out my hand and strike Egypt with all the wonders that I will do with it, after which he will let you go. And I will give these people favor in the sight of the Egyptians; when you go, you shall not go empty. How would God manifest such wonders? How could He mend the injustices, compensate for the losses, and pave the way for a fresh start? It was a question that resonated deeply, not just for the ancient Israelites but for me. How was He orchestrating a departure that left no void or emptiness but rather an abundance of promise? A spontaneous confession swelled within me instantly, a heartfelt plea to the heavens. 'I refuse to leave empty-handed, Father. Shower upon me a visitation that fills my barns with abundance in Jesus' name.'

Furthermore, in response, a serene peace enveloped me, a profound reminder that my departure was not a surrender but a transition. I was not departing devoid of riches – I carried the intangible gems of peace, dignity, an unblemished reputation, and cherished friendships. Though 'My Egypt' lay in the past, I embarked on this new chapter with dreams, visions, creative prowess, and the unwavering promises of God securely nestled within my being. As I stepped out of that elevator into a world free of 'My Egypt,' I realized that emptiness was not a void to be feared. I could not help but smile, infused with newfound excitement, as I ventured forward, leaving behind the familiar, embracing the unknown, and eagerly awaiting the wonders destined to fill my empty hands. As I walked away, the realization dawned upon me – it was not Egypt that had abandoned me; instead, I had boldly chosen to leave 'My Egypt.' This departure was not solely from a physical place; it was a liberation from self-imposed limits, a casting off of comfort's chains, and a leap into the vast expanse of possibilities. As I entered the unknown, I carried a treasury of treasures, each waiting to unfold and enrich my journey.

Activate Change

Break free from self-imposed limits, challenge the status quo, and pursue your dreams with unwavering determination. Take action by making conscious choices that align with your values and aspirations. Invite divine intervention into your journey. Through prayer, meditation, or spiritual practice, seek guidance and strength from a higher power.

Guided prayer

Lord, I pray for the courage to face challenges and uncertainties with determination, trusting in Your divine plan for our lives. Grant us the wisdom to embrace new opportunities and the strength to bid farewell to what is comfortable but no longer serves our purpose. Help us, Father, to welcome the wonders that life has in store, knowing that You are guiding our steps. Fill our hearts with hope and confidence as we navigate the uncharted path. May Your presence be a constant source of reassurance, reminding us that we are never alone in our journey. We surrender our fears and uncertainties to You, Lord, and trust that You will lead us with grace and purpose. Thank you for embracing change and the strength to face the unknown.

Affirmation

I am resilient, brave, and capable of embracing change.

Personalized Prayer and Reflection: [Your personalized prayer and reflection here]

_____

_____

_____

_____

_____

_____

_____

_____

_____

_____

_____

_____

_____

_____

_____

_____

Lorraine Murray-Richardson

WEEK 3- DAY 16

Faith Beyond Fear: Navigating the Unknown Path"

"The Egyptians you see today you will never see again."
Exodus 14:13

What would you do if you were not afraid? What dreams or goals have you put aside due to fear, and what could you achieve if you embraced the unknown with faith and courage?

_____

_____

_____

Embarking on a journey into unfamiliar terrain or facing the prospect of an unknown future is an unnerving challenge that tests the very core of our faith, pushing us to our limits. It is incredibly challenging to comprehend that God's plan remains the best for us, even in moments of disappointment. This truth becomes especially difficult to grasp when we have been fervently praying for a resounding 'yes' to the deepest desires of our hearts, much like my longing for a new job. However, instead of receiving a positive response, I encounter echoing rejections. The unpredictability of being jobless can evoke many emotions, ranging from anxiety to doubt, mirroring the Israelites' apprehensions as they gazed at the daunting expanse. Just as they pondered the uncertainties of their path, I found myself contemplating the tensions of my financial stability, daily routine, and a sense of purpose. The echoes of questions like 'What is next?' and 'Will I ever find another job?' reverberate, creating a constant sense of unease.

Similarly, the Israelites' journey through the Red Sea was an intimidating stretch spanning nine to twelve miles and plunging three hundred feet deep. This passage was no stroll; it was a treacherous obstacle that shook the Israelites to their core. Faced with such a formidable challenge, they found their instinctive fears taking hold, prompting them to express a preference for returning to their former enslavement rather than embracing God's plan for freedom. In their moment of crisis, they faltered in their trust in His love and purpose. It is tempting to judge the Israelites for wanting to turn back, especially considering the grueling slavery they left behind in Egypt and the promising future that lay ahead in the form of the coveted promised land.

The decision to keep moving forward might seem obvious, but in their defense, they were treading unfamiliar ground. The land showed no signs of the goodness they had been promised; it was unwelcoming and unfruitful. The promised land was not an immediate reality but a distant dream, making their journey daunting. The only reassurance they had was God saying, 'Move forward. Their longing for familiar comforts like meat, fish, cucumbers, melons, leeks, onions, and garlic was understandable. They yearned for what they did not have, seeking solace in the known rather than embracing the uncertainties of their current situation. I have found myself in a similar struggle. I was eager to regain the stability of having a job, to experience the simple joys of treating myself to something nice, traveling, and dining out spontaneously. However, all of these aspirations became obscured by the uncertainty brought about by my impulsive decision to resign from my job without a concrete plan in place. The familiarity of my past life, with its routines and comforts, started to appear appealing, just like the Israelites' yearning for the food and security they once knew.

Nevertheless, I, too, face the challenge of moving forward despite the uncertainties and embracing the unknown future. In the face of unknown waters, I recall God's resounding command to the Israelites: 'Move forward.' It is a message that resonates with me in my current circumstances, where the path ahead is shrouded in ambiguity and doubt.

Activate Change

Take proactive steps to navigate change with courage and determination, drawing strength from the lessons of the Israelites' journey. Instead of allowing fear to hinder your progress, seize this moment to embrace the unknown with open arms. Trust in your ability to adapt and thrive amidst uncertainty. Embrace change as an opportunity to redefine yourself and manifest the life you have always envisioned. The time for action is now. Step boldly into the future, empowered to activate change and chart a new course for your life.

Guided Prayer

Lord, I come to you seeking strength and guidance in moments of uncertainty and fear. As I stand at the crossroads of the unknown, I surrender my fears and doubts into your loving hands. Please grant me the courage to embrace the path ahead, even when I cannot see where it leads. Please help me find faith in my anxieties, trusting that your plan for me is far greater than any challenge I may face. Please give me the wisdom to discern my purpose and the patience to wait for the right opportunities to unfold. Let your light guide my steps, illuminating the way even in the darkest times. Help me overcome my longing for the familiar and grant me the strength to step out of my comfort zone. Please help me to find the resilience to navigate the uncertainties of life with grace and faith. As I move forward, I carry with me the echoes of your reassuring words: 'Move forward.' Bless me with the courage to heed this divine call, knowing that you are always with me, guiding my every step.

Affirmation

"I embrace the unknown with unwavering faith and courage."

Personalized Prayer and Reflection: [Your personalized prayer and reflection here]

_____

_____

_____

_____

_____

_____

_____

_____

_____

_____

_____

_____

_____

WEEK 3 - DAY 17

Melodies of Resilience: "Tuning into Hope, One Song at a Time"

"Then Moses and the Israelites sang this song to the Lord."
Exodus 15:1

Is there a particular song that serves as your anthem, motivating you and embodying the spirit of resilience, especially during challenging times?

_____

_____

_____

In the quiet moments of my life, I found myself drawn back to the story of the Israelites. They crossed the Red Sea on dry ground and witnessed their pursuers drowning at the place that had once instilled so much fear. Moses led them to safety in that very location, where they believed their lives would end, surrounded by Pharaoh's chariots. The song he led, echoing with gratitude for the enduring love of the Lord, became a battle cry, shattering the enemy's stronghold and paving the way for victory. As I faced my battles, I realized that singing became my sanctuary, even in my imperfect voice. It was not just about hitting the right notes; it was about pouring my heart and soul into the lyrics and finding strength in the melodies that resonated with my spirit. Music became my refuge, where fear and doubt melted away, replaced by a profound sense of peace and assurance. Much like the Israelites, my journey was fraught with fear and uncertainty. In moments of despair, when it seemed easier to succumb to the challenges, I remembered the triumphant song of Miriam and the women, celebrating their miraculous deliverance. Their music was more than just a jubilant celebration; it was a profound expression of gratitude, awe, and trust in the divine. As they stood on the dry ground, witnessing the miraculous parting of the sea, their hearts overflowed with a melody that transcended the limits of human language. It was a song of liberation, a tune that carried the weight of their enslavement in Egypt, the trials of the wilderness, and the unshakable faith in a God who had led them out of bondage.

Furthermore, the song of the Israelites was a proclamation of victory. They declared their triumph over fear, doubt, and despair with every note. The drowning of Pharaoh's army in the sea symbolized not just their physical liberation but also the defeat of their deepest fears and insecurities. Their song echoed with the confidence that as long as they remained faithful to their divine purpose, no enemy could prevail against them. In the depths of my struggles, I clung to the belief that just as God parted the Red Sea for the Israelites, He would make a way for me. With every note I sang, I felt His presence, guiding me through the storm, illuminating the path ahead. The melody became my prayer, a conversation with the divine, expressing my gratitude, fears, and hopes. Each song I sang became a testament to my faith, a declaration that despite the raging sea of uncertainties, I believed in a God who could calm the storm and lead me to the promised land. The lyrics became my anchor, grounding me in the assurance that no matter how fierce the battle, love would prevail, and light would pierce through the darkness. Thus, I sang. I sang with all my strength, channeling Miriam's jubilance, and the Israelites' unwavering faith. My voice may not have been perfect, but it became a powerful instrument in those moments, resonating with the melody of faith, echoing with the harmonies of hope, for all who listened. In life's storms, I discovered the transformative power of song – a beacon of hope, a lifeline that guided me and illuminated the path for others. Through the melodies, I found the courage to face my fears, the strength to overcome my challenges, and the inspiration to believe in the beauty of tomorrow. Moreover, in every note, a reminder was found that even in the face of adversity, there is a song within us waiting to be sung – a song of faith, hope, and belief in the enduring power of love.

Activate Change: In the symphony of life, much like a song that resonates with the soul, allow these treasures to harmonize with your spirit, infusing you with strength, resilience, and clarity of purpose. As you navigate the melody of change, let the harmonious chords of peace, dignity, integrity, and profound relationships be your guiding notes. Embrace these treasures as catalysts for transformation, empowering you to activate change and chart a new course with courage and conviction.

Guided Prayer

Lord, in moments of uncertainty and fear, I come before you, humbled and grateful for your unwavering love. Just as the Israelites trusted you at the Red Sea, I believe in your divine plan. Help me sing melodies of faith, even in the face of challenges. Please grant me the strength to harmonize with your grace, embracing the imperfect notes of my life as part of your divine composition. May my voice echo with gratitude and hope, affirming your presence in every circumstance. Lord, like the triumphant song of Miriam and the Israelites, let my prayers rise as melodies of resilience. In the music of my soul, dispel my fears and doubts, replacing them with your peace. Guide me through the storms, illuminating the path ahead with the light of your love. As I sing, let your melodies become my prayer, a conversation between our hearts. May my faith be a testament to your boundless grace, echoing your love into the world.

Affirmation

In the face of challenges, I sing melodies of faith.

Personalized Prayer and Reflection: [Your personalized prayer and reflection here]

_____

_____

_____

_____

_____

_____

_____

_____

_____

_____

_____

_____

_____

_____

_____

_____

WEEK 3 - DAY 18:

Thriving Through the Promised Land: "Unveiling My Survival Strategy"

"The LORD is my strength and defense[a];
he has become my salvation."
Exodus 15:2

What is your survival strategy that propels you forward instead of looking back when faced with challenges?

_____

_____

_____

Stepping out of the comforting familiarity of "My Egypt" into the vast, unknown landscape felt like taking a courageous leap of faith. However, the harsh reality of the economic challenges awaiting me on the other side made it seem like I had entered a nightmarish realm. As I sifted through online job listings, the modest incomes they offered sent shivers down my spine. The thought of embracing such meager salaries was a stark departure from anything I had ever known, making "My Egypt" suddenly appear as a haven of profitability. Leaving my job without a concrete plan was a bold move that required careful financial navigation to sustain my vulnerable household. Relying on two modest incomes and committing to frugal spending left no room for critical errors, let alone a decrease in earnings.

In a parallel narrative, the struggles the Children of Israel faced in the wilderness echoed my doubts and uncertainties. Despite witnessing miracles, their faith wavered. I found myself standing on similar ground, questioning the sufficiency of past provisions and yearning for a new deliverance. The echoes of their journey resonated with my own as I grappled with the uncertainty of my circumstances. Each passing day brought forth new challenges, and the allure of returning to the safety of "My Egypt" grew tempting. It was as if I were retracing the steps of those who had escaped the confines of their past only to find success on the outside. However, the weight of hopelessness settled upon me as the elusive success remained out of reach. In my uncertainty, the words of Exodus 5:12 echoed loudly in my mind. The vulnerability of the Israelites, unable to find the necessary materials for their bricks, resonated deeply. The image of them gathering stubble debris, scraping together what they could from the abundant land, mirrored my feelings of grasping at opportunities that seemed inadequate. The allure of "My Egypt" beckoned, promising a new seating area, better pay, and more work. Caught in this tug-of-war between my past and the unknown, I found my heart wavering between staying and leaving, much like the Israelites once faced.

The decision was not easy, and the path ahead remained unclear. However, in my indecisiveness, I held onto the belief that my journey was not in vain. Just as the Children of Israel found their way through the wilderness, I was determined to navigate the uncertainties and emerge on the other side, where the promise of a brighter future awaited. In the spirit of Moses, the leader of the Exodus, I decided to take charge of my destiny. Much like Moses parted the Red Sea, I needed to carve my path through the seemingly insurmountable challenges. I embraced the hardships as opportunities for growth and learning. Instead of seeing my circumstances as limiting, I started viewing them as a blank canvas upon which I could paint my dreams. Drawing from the Exodus story, I recognized the importance of community and support. Just as the Israelites leaned on each other during their journey, I sought mentors, friends, and allies who could bolster my spirits and offer guidance. Their encouragement became my pillar of strength, helping me face the challenges with renewed vigor. With each rejection in my job search, I gathered my metaphorical stubble debris, scraping together the bits of courage, determination, and hope I could find within myself. Once terrifying, the vast unknown became a canvas upon which I could paint my dreams. Instead of seeing my circumstances as limiting, I started viewing them as a blank slate, ready to be filled with the colors of my aspirations.

As I continued my job search, I adopted the determination of the Israelites building their bricks under duress. Each rejection became a lesson, a stepping stone towards a more resilient version of myself. I honed my skills, expanded my horizons, and embraced every opportunity for personal and professional development. The setbacks no longer discouraged me; they fueled my determination to prove my worth in the competitive landscape I found myself in. I discovered an inner strength that I never knew existed in the heart of my struggle. Much like the trials the Children of Israel faced, adversity became the crucible that forged my resilience. I refused to succumb to despair, seeing my journey as a testament to the human spirit's ability to endure and overcome. With time, my persistence began to bear fruit. I secured a job that, while not immediately resembling the safety of "My Egypt," held the promise of growth and opportunity. The initial modest income became a stepping stone, a foundation upon which I could build a stable future for my family. The sacrifices I made and the risks I took started to make sense as I saw the first signs of success on the horizon. Looking back, I realized that my journey mirrored the Exodus in more ways than one. It was a passage from the familiar confines of complacency to the vast expanse of possibilities. The challenges I faced, and the doubts that haunted me faded into the background as I embraced the promise of a brighter future. Just like the Israelites found their way to the promised land,

I, too, had reached a place of stability and contentment. The courage to leave "My Egypt" and face the unknown transformed my life and became a testament to the power of faith, resilience, and unwavering determination. Much like the Exodus, my story reminded me that even in the face of seemingly insurmountable odds, the human spirit could triumph, leading the way to a better tomorrow.

Activate Change

Activate change by advocating for a radical shift in your perspective. Take a bold step by questioning your current mindset and beliefs. Examine why you think and act the way you do. Consider alternative viewpoints and be open to radical shifts in your perspective. Embrace your failures, successes, and disappointments—the entire gamut of what shapes your past and future. Instead of dwelling on your past, focus on moving forward to your future.

Guided prayer

In this moment of uncertainty, I humbly come before you, recognizing the parallels between my journey and the Exodus of the Children of Israel. As you become a defense and savior to the Israelites in their time of need, I seek your guidance, strength, and protection as I navigate the challenges. Grant me the courage to face the unknown with faith and resilience, knowing that you are always by my side, just as you were with the Israelites during their journey through the wilderness. Help me trust your plan, even when the path ahead seems unclear. Fill my heart with hope and perseverance, knowing that with your help, I can endure and overcome any obstacle that stands in my way. Let your light shine upon me, illuminating the darkness of doubt and fear and leading me toward a brighter future. May I find solace in your presence, knowing that you are my refuge and strength in times of trouble. Help me to lean on you for support, just as the Israelites leaned on you during their Exodus journey. In your infinite mercy and grace, guide me along the path of righteousness and grant me the peace that surpasses all understanding. Amen.

Affirmation

I am resilient, courageous, and capable of overcoming any challenge that comes my way.

Personalized Prayer and Reflection: [Your personalized prayer and reflection here]

_____

_____

_____

_____

_____

_____

_____

_____

_____

_____

_____

_____

_____

WEEK 3- DAY 19

Beyond Egypt's Bounds: "Letting Go Forever"

*Forget the former things; do not dwell on the past. See, I am
doing a new thing! Now it springs up; do you not perceive it? I am
making a way in the wilderness and streams in the wasteland."
Isaiah 43:18-19 (NIV)*

**"Reflecting on your journey, consider this: What empowering
beliefs or positive affirmations can you embrace to help you let
go permanently?**

_____

_____

_____

In the final chapter of my Exodus from Egypt, I find myself standing
at the crossroads of my past and the promising future that awaits me.
The journey to abandon Egypt was not merely a physical relocation
but a profound spiritual and emotional transformation. It was about
shedding the heavy layers of doubt, fear, and complacency that had
held me captive for far too long. As I bid farewell to the familiarity
of my Egypt, gratitude fills me for the lessons learned, the obstacles
overcome, and the person I have become. Leaving Egypt was a leap
of faith, a courageous step into the unknown driven by a deep inner
calling for change and growth.

Uncertainties strewn the path, and challenges and setbacks frequently
obscured the road to my promised land. There were moments of

doubt when I questioned the wisdom of my decision and the strength of my resolve. However, in those moments of darkness, I found a flicker of light within me – a beacon of hope and determination that guided me forward. Abandoning Egypt meant breaking free from the chains of my limitations. It declared my worthiness for a life filled with abundance, joy, and fulfillment. With each step away from the past, I embraced the boundless possibilities of the future. I learned that true liberation comes from within, from the courage to confront my fears and the willingness to trust the journey. This Exodus was a transformative process that demanded resilience and unwavering faith. It required me to confront my deepest fears and insecurities, to challenge the status quo, and to dare greatly. Through trials and tribulations, I discovered the depths of my strength and the vastness of my potential. I realized that my definition is not rooted in past circumstances but in my choices in the present and my vision for my future. As I stand on the threshold of this new chapter, I carry with me the wisdom gained from abandoning Egypt. I understand that life's journey is not always linear; it is a series of twists and turns, ups and downs. Each obstacle I faced and every moment of doubt I conquered has shaped me into a stronger, more resilient individual. I have learned that setbacks are not failures but opportunities for growth and self-discovery. They are the stepping stones that lead me closer to my dreams. In embracing the fullness of life's possibilities, I step into the embrace of a promising future. The unwavering faith that carried me through the darkest nights and the resilience that lifted me in the face of adversity inspires me. Leaving Egypt was not an act of abandonment but a triumphant declaration of my inherent power and worth. As I move forward, I do so with gratitude for the journey behind me and excitement for the adventures ahead. I am no longer bound by the limitations of my past but propelled by the limitless potential within me. I am ready to conquer new horizons, embrace new challenges, and create a life that reflects my true essence. With a heart full of gratitude and a spirit ablaze with determination, I step confidently into the unknown, knowing that the best is yet to come. My Exodus from Egypt was not just a chapter in my life; it was a testament to the power of faith, resilience, and unwavering belief in the endless possibilities that await those who dare to dream.

Activate Change

To activate change and confront your personal Egypt, start your day by affirming your worthiness and potential. Positive affirmations like "I am capable of greatness" or "I embrace change and growth" can profoundly shift your mindset, instilling confidence and propelling you forward. Additionally, cultivate a supportive network of friends, family, and mentors who can offer encouragement and guidance. This support system motivates you to overcome challenges and focus on your goals.

Guided Prayer

In this moment of gratitude and humility, I come before you with a heart of thanksgiving for the journey that has brought me to this place."

I stand on the threshold of new beginnings, leaving behind the familiar comforts of my past, just as the Children of Israel left Egypt. I am in awe of the lessons learned, the strength discovered, and the faith renewed during this transformative journey. I surrender my fears and doubts at your feet, acknowledging that your divine wisdom guides my path. As I embark on this new chapter, I seek your guidance and blessings. Grant me the courage to embrace the unknown, just as Moses led his people through the wilderness. Infuse me with the determination to overcome obstacles and the resilience to face challenges gracefully. I am grateful for the freedom to let go of the limitations that have bound me, the opportunity to abandon the fears that held me back, and the chance to rediscover the essence of who I am. I trust your divine plan and timing, believing that your loving hands orchestrate every twist and turn in my journey. I pray for strength, patience, and perseverance to weather the storms that may come my way.

Fill my heart with faith, hope, and love so I may navigate this new path with grace and confidence. Help me recognize the opportunities disguised as challenges and the blessings hidden within difficulties. Guide me toward meaningful connections and supportive relationships, just as the Israelites found community in their fellow travelers. Surround me with mentors and companions who uplift my spirit and inspire me to become the best version of myself. May their wisdom be a guiding light, illuminating my way forward. I acknowledge the power of my thoughts and intentions. I affirm my worthiness of all the blessings you have in store for me. Help me cultivate a mindset of abundance, gratitude, and positivity so that I may attract blessings and miracles into my life. Strengthen my belief in my abilities and remind me that I can achieve my dreams. I surrender my desires and aspirations to you, trusting you to know what is best for me. Lord, may my journey be aligned with your divine purpose, and may I be a vessel of your love, compassion, and kindness in the world. Grant me the wisdom to discern your guidance and the courage to follow it with an open heart.

Affirmation

I release the chains of my past, bidding farewell to Egypt's familiar embrace. I no longer let the limitations that once held me captive confine me. I embrace the unknown with unwavering courage, stepping into the boundless possibilities beyond Egypt's bounds.

Personalized Prayer and Reflection: [Your personalized prayer and reflection here]

WEEK 3- DAY 20

"Pressing Forward: Embrace the Journey, Do not Look Back"

"Why do you cry out to me? Tell the
people of Israel to go forward."
Exodus 14:15 (NIV)

"What does it mean to wait on God indeed, and how does the experience of waiting shape our understanding of His character and our relationship with Him?

_____

_____

_____

In this season of my journey, I am reminded of the anticipation felt on an airplane as it ascends toward its destination. Despite the breathtaking views and dreams of the destination, obstacles such as other aircraft or turbulent weather may prolong the journey and arrive seem agonizingly distant. The desire to take control and hasten the journey is intense within me. I am not one to sit idly by; I am accustomed to taking action, fixing problems, and making things happen. The sight of the promised land in the distance only exacerbates my impatience. I have already waited so long, and waiting any longer feels intolerable. As the Children of Israel stood facing the formidable barrier of the Red Sea, doubt crept into their hearts, questioning whether God truly had their best interests at heart. The path carved through the sea, stretching nine to twelve miles in length and plunging three hundred feet into its depths, presented a daunting challenge, far from a simple stroll.

Confronted with such adversity, the people voiced their fears, expressing a longing to retreat to the familiarity of bondage, a stark rejection of God's love and His plan for their freedom. It is easy to pass judgment on the Israelites for their desire to return to the comfort of slavery. Along my journey, I have felt the tug of my metaphorical Egypt. It beckons with familiarity, offering respite from the uncertainty the Red Sea symbolizes. Psalms 25:8-10 acknowledges the reality of these feelings of uncertainty and fear but also provides reassurance that the Lord guides those who stray onto the right path with His unfailing love and faithfulness. The reminder that it was God who set me on this path brings a measure of comfort, although sobering, reminding me that my life is not entirely my own and that everything unfolds in His perfect timing. Embracing God's invitation to trust in His plans for the present and His faithfulness for the future requires complete reliance on His word, truth, and promises.

Interestingly, God chose not to lead the Israelites through the shortest route to their destination but instead guided them on a path of growth and preparation for the journey ahead. He understood that the shortest path often leads back to the bondage they sought to escape. The journey away from our metaphorical "Egypt" is undeniably challenging. Like the Israelites facing the Red Sea, we encounter obstacles that test our faith, push us to our limits, and tempt us to retreat to the familiarity of what we once knew. However, just as the Israelites found liberation on the other side of the sea, we, too, can discover true freedom, growth, and fulfillment when we press forward on our journey. Returning to Egypt, though it may seem easier in moments of doubt or hardship, ultimately leads us back to bondage. It confines us to the limitations of our past, stifles our growth, and prevents us from realizing our full potential. While the path forward may be uncertain and tense with challenges, it is also filled with promise, opportunity, and the potential for transformation. Resisting the urge to revert to our Egypt requires courage, perseverance, and unwavering faith. It means trusting God's plan, even when unclear or daunting. It means embracing discomfort and uncertainty as necessary steps toward growth and fulfillment. It means recognizing that true freedom lies not in looking back but in pressing forward despite the obstacles that may lie ahead. Though the journey from Egypt may be harrowing, it is undoubtedly worth it. It leads us to a place of greater purpose, authenticity, and abundance. It allows us to break free from the chains of our past and step into the fullness of who we were created to be. So let us not be swayed by the allure of what once was but press forward with courage and conviction, knowing that the best is yet to come.

Activate Change

Waiting upon God is not passive but an active posture of the heart. It is a deliberate choice to relinquish our agenda and align ourselves with His will. It is an opportunity to grow in intimacy with Him, deepen our understanding of His character, and cultivate a spirit of humility and dependence. While waiting may feel uncomfortable and uncertain, it is in waiting that God often does His most profound work within us. He shapes and molds us, refining our character, strengthening our faith, and preparing us for the journey. Trust that God is at work, even when His plans seem hidden. Moreover, the waiting may be challenging, but it is worth it. In the waiting, we discover the beauty of God's timing and the richness of His presence.

As you wait:

Psalm 37:34 - "Wait for the LORD and keep His way, And He will exalt you to inherit the land; when the wicked are cut off, you will see it."

Lamentations 3:25 - "The LORD is good to those who wait for Him, to the person who seeks Him."

Numbers 9:8 - "Moses, therefore, said to them, 'Wait and I will listen to what the LORD will command concerning you.

Guided Prayer

Lord, I confess that waiting is not easy for me. Often, I find myself restless, anxious, and eager to take matters into my own hands. However, I know Your ways are higher than mine, and Your timing is perfect. Today, I surrender my impatience and desire for control into Your loving hands. Help me, Lord, to wait upon You with trust and confidence. Teach me to align my will with Yours and find peace knowing that You are always at work, even when Your plans seem hidden. Please grant me the grace to embrace this season of waiting as an opportunity for growth and transformation. May it be a time of deepening intimacy with You as I draw closer to Your heart and seek to understand Your character more fully. Lord, strengthen my faith during this time of waiting. Help me to believe wholeheartedly in Your promises, knowing that You are faithful in fulfilling them in Your perfect timing. Give me the patience to endure and the courage to persevere, trusting that You are leading me toward a future filled with hope and purpose. May Your peace, wisdom, and presence surround me as I await You. Help me to rest in Your love, knowing that You are always with me, guiding me every step of the way. Thank you, Lord, for Your goodness, faithfulness, and unfailing love. May my waiting be a testimony to Your grace and Your sovereignty.

In Jesus' name, Amen."

Affirmation

I will wait on the Lord and take heart, knowing my strength is renewed as I trust His perfect timing and faithfulness.

Personalized Prayer and Reflection: [Your personalized prayer and reflection here]

_____

_____

_____

_____

_____

_____

_____

_____

_____

_____

_____

_____

WEEK 3- DAY 21

Embracing Freedom:
"The Final Step of Abandoning Egypt"

*"I will bring you to the land I swore with uplifted hand to give to
Abraham, Isaac, and Jacob. I will give it to you as a possession."*
Exodus 6:8

As we conclude this transformative journey, I invite you to engage in
a reflective activity to solidify the lessons learned and inspire your
growth beyond these pages. Find a quiet, comfortable space to be
alone with your thoughts and emotions.

Reflect: Take a few moments to ponder the critical themes of this
book. Consider the challenges faced by the characters, the lessons
they learned, and the courage they exhibited. Think about your own
life and the parallels you find with their journey. What aspects of your
life resemble your "Egypt"? What fears and doubts keep you from
embracing change and pursuing your dreams?

_____

_____

_____

_____

_____

Identify Your Exodus Moments: Recall moments when you exhibited resilience, courage, or determination. These are your own "Exodus moments." They can be significant achievements or small victories when you overcome adversity or step out of your comfort zone.

Define Your Promised Land: Envision the life you want to create beyond your limitations. What does your promised land look like? What are your dreams, goals, and aspirations? How do you want to feel, and what impact do you want to make?

_____

_____

_____

_____

_____

Write Your Manifesto: Craft your personal Exodus Manifesto. Write a heartfelt declaration of your intentions to leave behind what no longer serves you and embrace the boundless opportunities of the future. Be specific about the changes you wish to make and the person you aspire to become. Use affirmative language and infuse your manifesto with passion and determination.

_____

_____

_____

_____

_____

_____

Visualize: After writing your manifesto, take a moment to close your eyes and visualize yourself living the life described in your manifesto. Feel the emotions associated with your achievements, immerse yourself in the sense of accomplishment, and let this visualization empower you.

Take Action: Commit to taking one actionable step toward your goals within the next 24 hours. It can be a small step, but it should align with the principles of your manifesto. Whether reaching out to a mentor, signing up for a course, or positively changing your routine, taking action will solidify your commitment to your Exodus journey.

Remember, this manifesto is a living document. Revisit it regularly, revise it as needed, and let it guide you toward personal transformation. Embrace your own Exodus journey with confidence.

Thank you for the strength to abandon my Egypt and for the promise of a brighter tomorrow. I surrender my journey into your loving hands.

ABOUT THE AUTHOR

 Lorraine Murray Richardson is an avid reader, especially books that encourage individuals how to live a bold and, God centered life. She believes God has so much more, He want to say to his people including through books which are timeless and are relevant in every generation. Writing books that are inspiring, and relatable was always on her bucket list, "Abandoning Egypt is the birth of that reality. She is also a wife and the mother of two wonderful children and a niece whom she adores. She has serve as the Director of Children Ministries for the last 13 years under the Leadership of Pastor Carl and Reva Richardson of Living Hope Cathedral in St. Thomas United States Virgin Islands.

Printed in the United States
by Baker & Taylor Publisher Services